Empire

ORIGINAL SOUNDTRACK FROM SEASON 1

ISBN 978-1-4950-2256-2

HAL•LEONARD®
CORPORATION
7777 W. BLUEMOUND RD. P.O. BOX 13819 MILWAUKEE, WI 53213

Visit Hal Leonard Online at
www.halleonard.com

GOOD ENOUGH

Words and Music by DANIEL JONES,
JAMES DAVID WASHINGTON and TIMBALAND

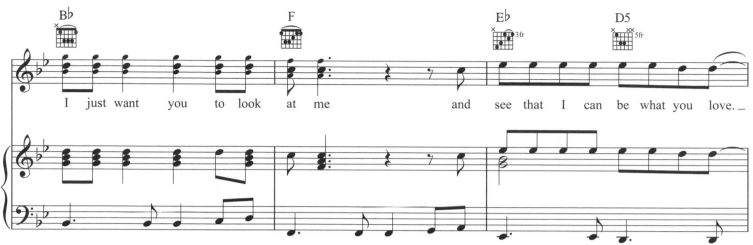

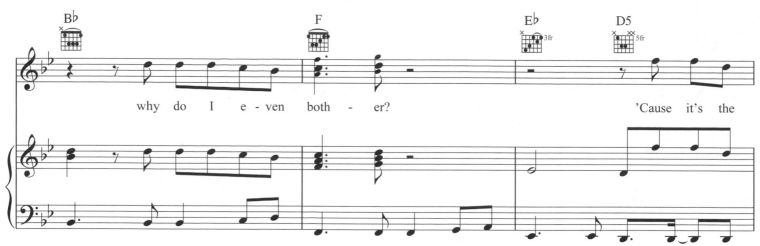

why do I e-ven both-er? 'Cause it's the

same ol' damn ___ song, you call your-self a fa-ther, whoa. ___

___ Feel like I'm reach-in' for the stars, ___ but heav-en is-n't

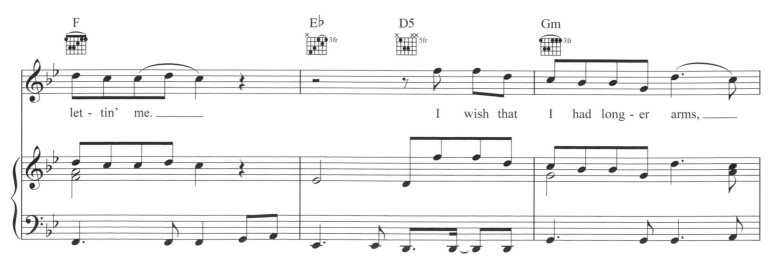

let-tin' me. ___ I wish that I had long-er arms, ___

you give a damn? (Look at me.) See, it does-n't mat-

-ter what you think, I'm still a man. (Look at me.)

O - pen up your eyes, can't you see that I'm good e-

nough? Whoa, look at (I just want you to look at me.)

me _____

I just want you to look at me. _____

See that I can be _____ good e - nough, good e - nough,

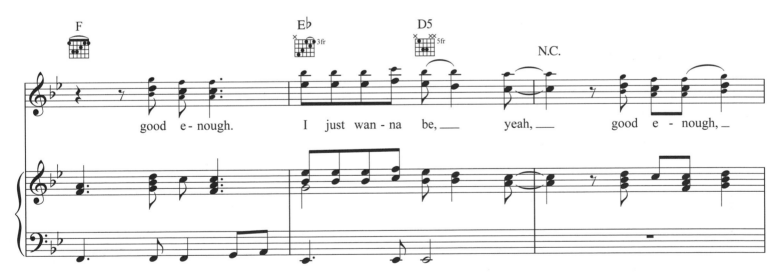

good e - nough. I just wan - na be, ___ yeah, ___ good e - nough, __

good e - nough, __ good e - nough, _____ good e - nough.

WHAT IS LOVE?

Words and Music by DANIEL JONES,
JAMES DAVID WASHINGTON, TIMBALAND
and VERONIKA BOZEMAN

Heavy R&B Ballad

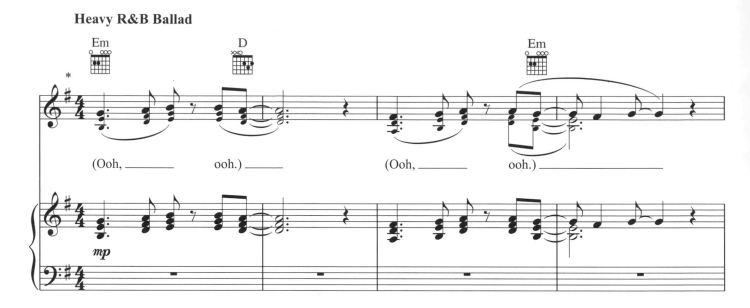

(Ooh, _____ ooh.) _____   (Ooh, _____ ooh.) _____

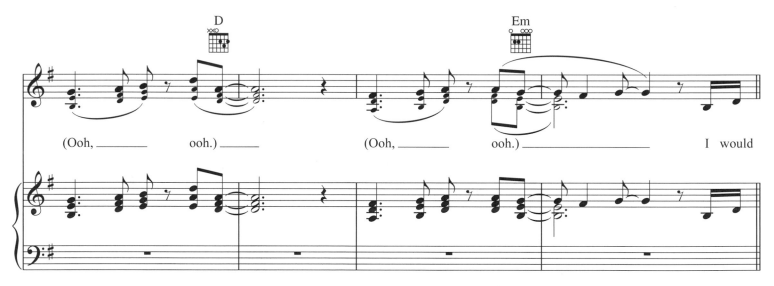

(Ooh, _____ ooh.) _____   (Ooh, _____ ooh.) _____   I would

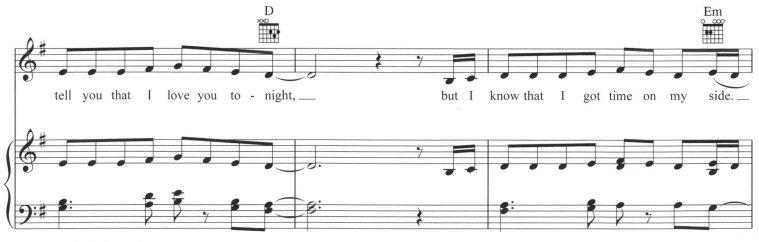

tell you that I love you to-night, ___ but I know that I got time on my side.

* *Recorded a half step lower.*

Where you go- in'? Why you leav- in' so soon? _____ Is there

some- where else that's bet- ter for you? _____ What is love _____ if you're not here _

_ with me? _ What is love _____ if it's not guar - an - teed? _ What is love _

_ if it just up and leaves? _____ Ooh, _ what is love _____ if you're not here _

no more? What is love ___ if you're not real - ly sure? ___ What is love? ___

___ What is love? ___ Tell my - self I would-n't cry when you're gone, ___

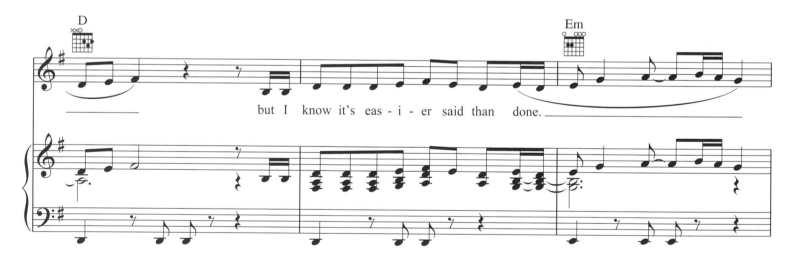

___ but I know it's eas - i - er said than done. ___

Look at me, look at me, choked up now. ___ Try to tell you, but it won't come

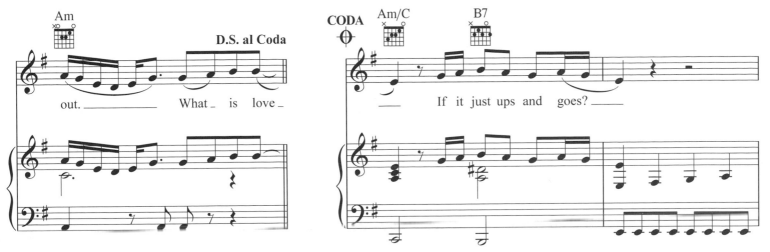

D.S. al Coda

Am

out. ___ What is love ___

CODA

Am/C   B7

___ If it just ups and goes? ___

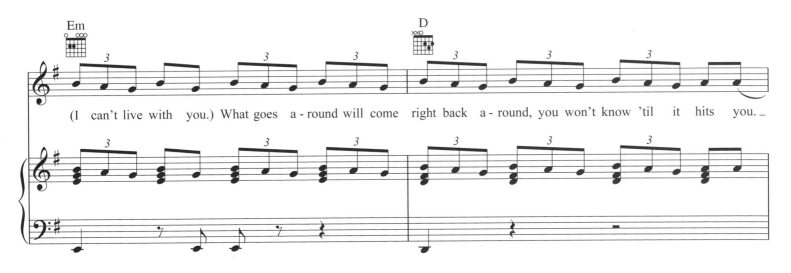

Am   B5

I can't live with-out you. (Can't live with-out you.) I can't live with you.

Em   D

(I can't live with you.) What goes a-round will come right back a-round, you won't know 'til it hits you. ___

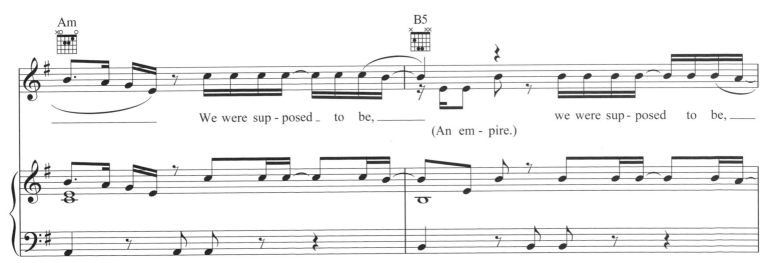

Am   B5

___ We were sup-posed ___ to be, ___ we were sup-posed to be, ___

(An em - pire.)

we were sup-posed to be _____ an em-pire. What is love _____ if you're not here _
(An em-pire.)

_ with me? What is love _____ if it's not guar - an - teed? _ What is love_

_ if it just up and leaves? _____ What is love? _____ What is love _

_ if you're not real - ly sure? _ What is love _____ if it just ups? _

NO APOLOGIES

Words and Music by JAMES DAVID WASHINGTON
and TIMBALAND

Spoken: Uh huh.

(Turn it up, turn it, turn it, turn it, hell yeah, hell yeah.) My mouth is a weap-on. I ain't scared of noth-in'. They say he so reck-less, bunk-ie in the cas-ket. Bet-ter hit the

* *Recorded a half step lower.*

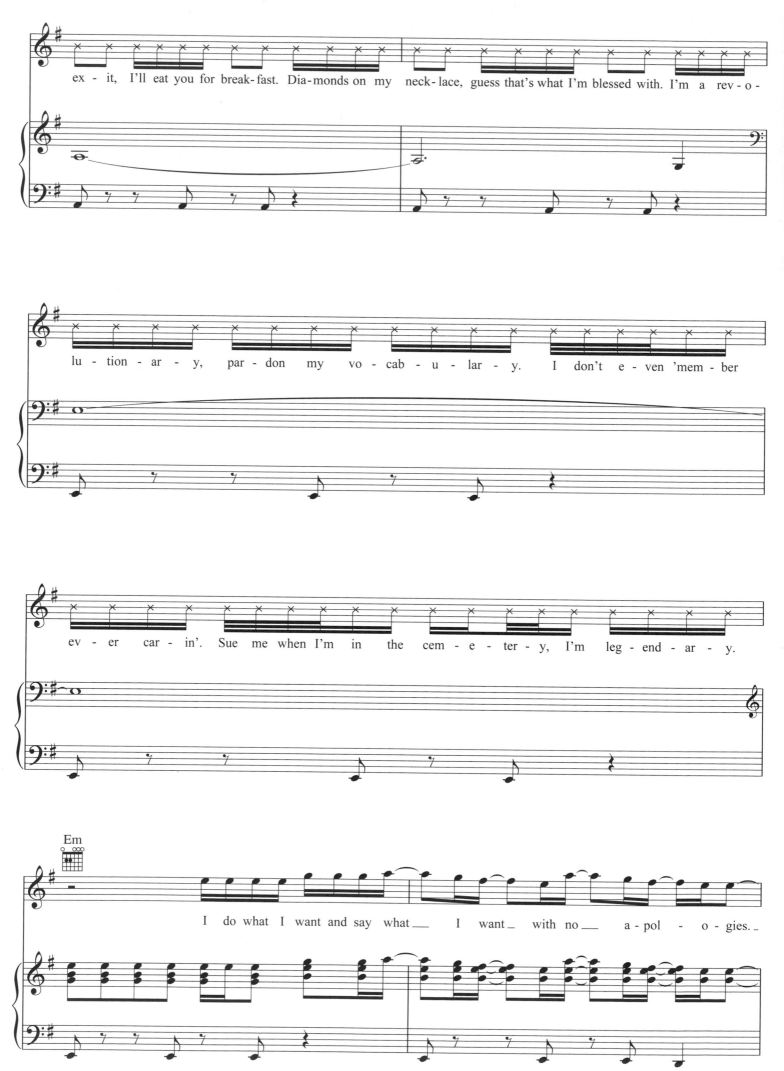

Ex-cuse me if I'm blunt, I say what___ I want___ with no___ a - pol - o - gies.___

And they won't shut me up, hell naw, hell naw. And they won't shut me up, hell naw,

hell naw. I do what I want and say what___ I want___ with no___ a - pol - o - gies.___

They get mad, I keep on talk-in'. Nev-er mind, I beg your par-don. Guess I'm just too damn out - spo-ken. They can't take me an-y-where.

com-in' for ya,   hope you're read-y.   Read-y,   aim,   fi-re, fi-re, leg-en-dar-y.

(Gun-nin' for ya,   au-to-mat-ic,   read-y,   aim,   fi-re, leg-en-dar-y.)

Oh.   I do what I want and say what __ I want __ with no __ a-pol-o-gies. __

Ex-cuse me if I'm blunt, I say what __ I want __ with no __ a-pol-o-gies. __

And they won't shut me up, hell naw,   hell naw.   And they won't shut me up, hell naw,

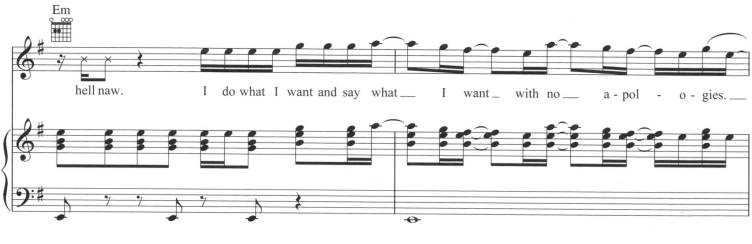

hell naw.   I do what I want and say what __ I want __ with no __ a - pol - o - gies. __

(Rap continues in triplet rhythm)

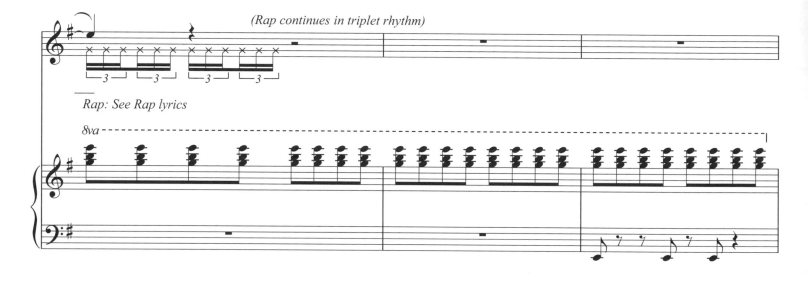

Rap: See Rap lyrics

8va

I ain't sor - ry,   I ain't sor - ry for noth - in' I said. __

Em/C

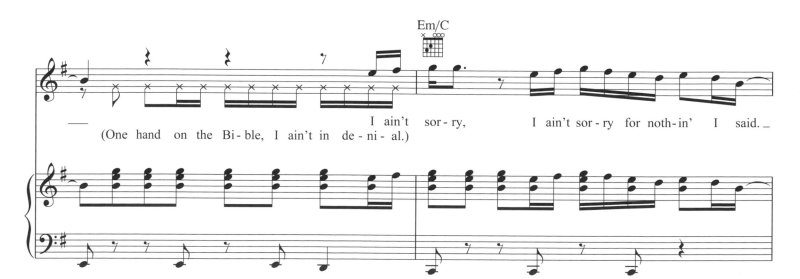

I ain't sor - ry,   I ain't sor - ry for noth - in' I said. __
(One hand on the Bi - ble, I ain't in de - ni - al.)

Additional Lyrics

Rap: They can't be mad at me, look at my family.
I guess it's all in my blood line.
If you keep ridin' me for my apology,
You'll be waitin' for a long time.
Not sympathetic, I said it, I meant it.
You don't like it, then I could care less.
Not sympathetic, I said it, I meant it.
You don't like it, then I could care less.

KEEP IT MOVIN'

Words and Music by JAMES DAVID WASHINGTON
and TIMBALAND

Latin-flavored Hip-Hop

Oh, _____ keep it mov-in', here we go. Keep it mov-in', here we

go go go go go go go go go. Bod-y like a weap-on. It goes ba-ba-ba - bang bang. And ev-'ry

Play 4 times

time that we're to-geth-er, I make you ___ say my name.

(Bounce.) *Yeah.* (Bounce.)

WALK OUT ON ME

Words and Music by SEAN VAN VLEET
and CHARLES WRIGHT

Walk out on me, walk out on me,__ I'll see you for the last__ time.__

__ Walk out on me, walk out on me,_ I'm giv-in' you a life - line.__ Say__ so long,__

__ and then walk a-way. Say__ so long,_____ and then walk a-way.

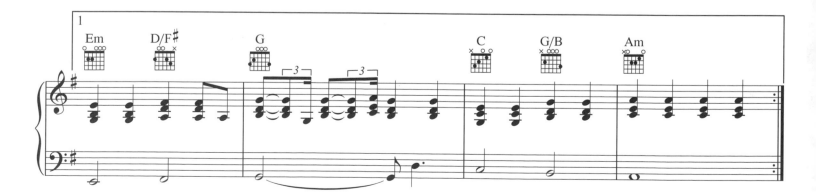

CONQUEROR

Words and Music by AKIL KING, KYLE OWENS,
JOHN LARDIERI, JARAMYE DANIELS, CLAUDE KELLY,
ESTELLE SWARAY, SHARIF SLATER and ANGEL HIGGS

Well, we all___ make mis-takes.___ You might fall___ on your face,_____ but you got-ta get

up._____ *Girl:* I'd rath-er stand tall___ than live on my knees,_ 'cause I am a con-

- quer-or,_____ and I won't ac-cept___ de-feat._____ Try tell-in' me

no._____ One thing a-bout me____ is I am a con-

Am   Am/G   F   Gsus

- quer - or, _____ I am a con - quer - or, _____ oh. ____

C   Em/B

Got a vis - ion that no one else sees. Lot of dirt - y work, roll up your

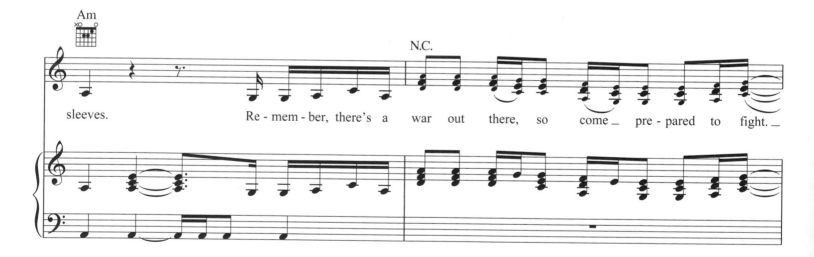

Am   N.C.

sleeves. Re - mem - ber, there's a war out there, so come __ pre - pared to fight. __

C   Em/B

_____ You nev - er know where the road leads you. Not ev - 'ry - one's gon - na be -

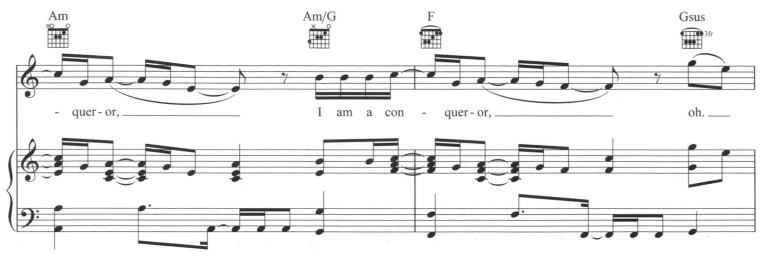

quer - or, _____ I am a con - quer - or, _____ oh. ___

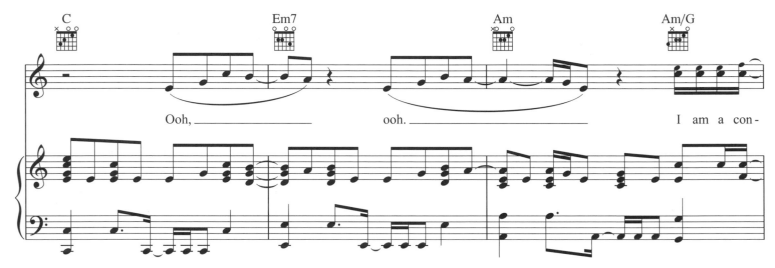

Ooh, _____ ooh. _____ I am a con-

To Coda ⊕

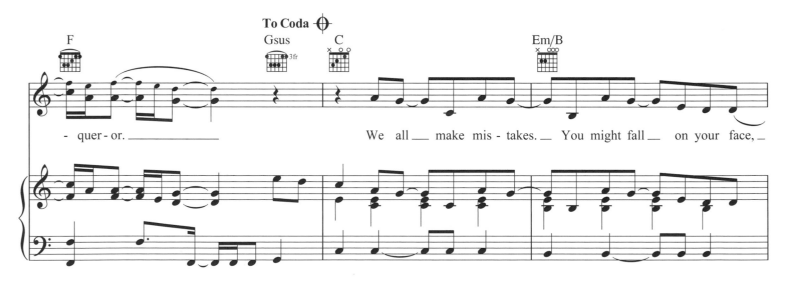

quer - or. _____ We all __ make mis - takes. __ You might fall __ on your face, __

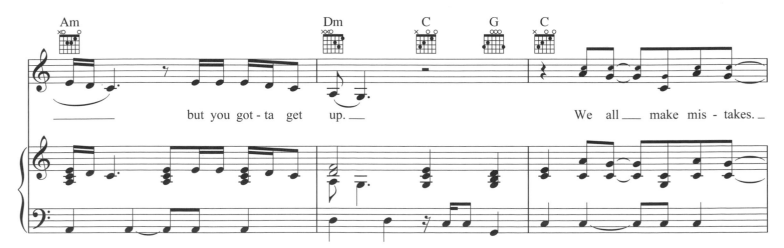

_____ but you got - ta get up. __ We all __ make mis - takes. __

D.S. al Coda

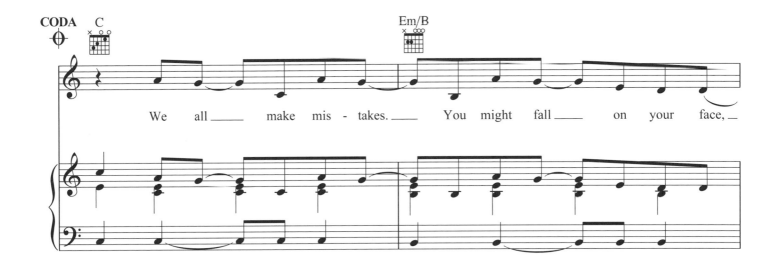

You might fall ___ on your face. _____ Don't ev-er give up. _____ I'd rath-er stand

CODA

We all ___ make mis - takes. ___ You might fall ___ on your face, ___

___ but I am a con - quer - or. ___

REMEMBER THE MUSIC

Words and Music by JAMES DAVID WASHINGTON
and JUSTIN BOSTWICK

R&B Ballad

* Recorded a half step higher.

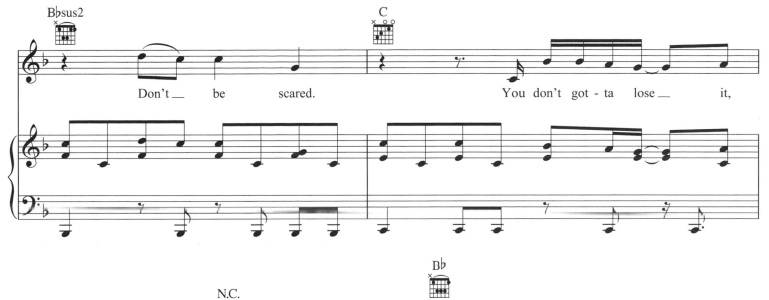

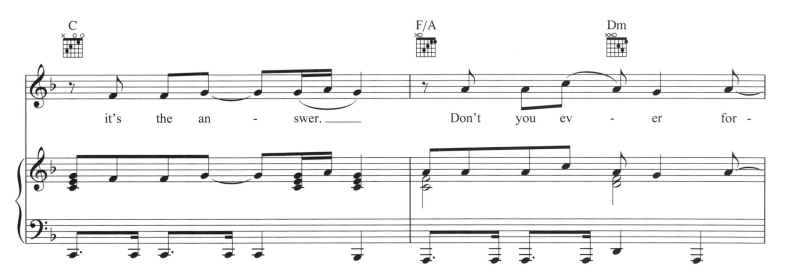

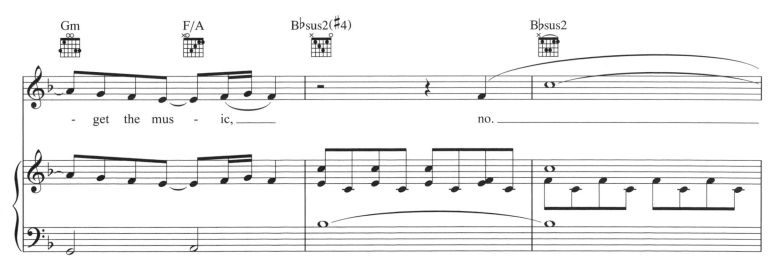

SHAKE DOWN

Words and Music by CHRISTOPHER "TRICKY" STEWART,
TERIUS NASH, PHALON ALEXANDER
and USHER RAYMOND

Flowing R&B

*Originally recorded a half step lower.

(Babe, you gon-na give me all your love to-night. Don't you hes-i-tate, ba-by, don't put up a fight.)

shake down.) ('Cause it's a

shake down, shake down. Shake down, shake down.) _____

Repeat and Fade

Additional lyrics

Rap: Love up in the air, baby girl runs my heartstrings.
Don't forget where ya play it, baby doll face.
Make that solemn break, make the vow shake.
Later, we get rich, make the wild habit.
Seem like modern hoodstas, and then they shoot ya.
Ready, aim and fire, play hard, retire.
Lock, stock and barrel, straight path, and narrow.
Shake it down forever, why, when, whatever.

POWER OF THE EMPIRE

Words and Music by JAMES DAVID WASHINGTON
and JUSTIN BOSTWICK

Recorded a half step lower.

see me ball, peo-ple will nev-er see me fall 'cause I got the   For the

pow - er.   For the pow - er.
pow - er.   (For the pow - er.)   (All __

D.S. al Coda

CODA

__ for the pow - er.)   For the

Lie, cheat, __ steal, __ fight,

N.C.

(I'll do an - y-thing for the pow - er.)

just to get home for the night. __   Li-, li-, lie, cheat, __

steal, ___ fight, just to get home for the night. ___ (I'll do an - y - thing for the pow -

- er.) I want ev - 'ry - bod - y at at - ten - tion. You could call me Mis - ter

(I'll do an - y - thing for the pow - er.) If mon - ey is the root to all e - vil, you can
Ly - on when I vis - it.

see me ball, peo - ple will nev - er see me fall 'cause I got the pow - er.

NOTHING TO LOSE

Words and Music by JAMES DAVID WASHINGTON
and TIMBALAND

whoa. At least I don't have to wor-ry a-bout the fall.

D.S. al Coda

Why did I end up with nine - ty-nine prob-lems?

CODA

N.C.

WHATEVER MAKES YOU HAPPY

Words and Music by JAMES DAVID WASHINGTON
and JENNIFER HUDSON

*Recorded a half step lower.